Poetry For Christmas
Twelve Poems For Mid-Winter

Chosen & Introduced
by
Orna Ross

Font Publications

Contents

Introduction	1
"The Nativity of our Lord and Saviour Jesus Christ." Christopher Smart.	15
"Christmas." John Betjeman.	17
"The Oxen." By Thomas Hardy.	19
"Christmas Poem." Mary Oliver.	21
"Noel." By Anne Porter.	23
"The Magi". W.B. Yeats.	25
"Journey Of The Magi." T.S. Eliot.	27
"Christmas Time." Dan Holloway.	29
"Translations." Adrienne Rich.	31
"Christmas Eve." Anne Sexton.	33
"A Christmas Childhood." Patrick Kavanagh.	35
"A Christmas Oratorio". W.H. Auden.	37
- Conclusion: Blessing	41
"Mid-Winter Benediction." Orna Ross.	43
About The Poets.	45
About The Editor.	47

Introduction

Everyday language, Flaubert once said, is "a cracked kettle on which we tap crude rhythms for bears to dance to — while we long to make music that will melt the stars". Poetry is words artfully and musically arranged and good poetry compresses the art and music to that star-melting point.

That's why reading a poem a day has a transforming effect on our lives. It's not just that lovingly crafted words elevate our existence, meeting our need for beauty, grace and meaning. What's equally at play is the act of making poetry a priority in our lives, acknowledging that neglected need and making space to meet it; taking the time to open the head, and heart and yes, the soul, whatever that might be and however we understand it, in order to indulge this serious pleasure.

This commitment, the giving of this pleasure to ourselves, as much as the words themselves, is what allows poetry to melt and meld and mould us for the better.

The mid-winter holiday season provides the perfect space to make daily poetry a habit. Long nights under lamplight, with a fire or candle flickering and a favorite beverage within arm's reach, provide the perfect conditions for new adventures in language and learning.

In this pamphlet, you'll find a poem for each of the traditional twelve days of christmas. They all relate in some way to the story we've been telling for 2000 years about what happened in Bethlehem on a certain 25th December. Some of the poems reassert that story, some challenge it, some see it as purely symbolic — but all are engaged with the deeper questions that underwrite it.

These questions fired pre-christian versions of the midwinter tale, which were gathered into the story of Jesus, and they still interrogate secular, post-christian life. Questions like: What is god? What does it mean for me if I believe in that entity? If I don't? What is this light we so long for in our dark moments, that these poets seek and express here, that the christmas story symbolises? Where does it come from? In the heart of darkness, how can we find it?

In *Hamlet*, Shakespeare described christmas as a time when night is "wholesome... so hallowed and so gracious" that "... no spirit dare stir abroad...no planets strike,/no fairy takes, nor witch hath power to charm." The fears and frights of the dark cannot find a foothold in this night so silent and so holy, where all is calm, and bright, sleeping in heavenly peace.

On such a night, the christian story tells, Jesus was born, in a lowly stable, son of an unmarried virgin-mother. He and she together symbolise the opposite of the worldly, material power of the father. Female and child, humble and holy, meek and mild though vulnerable, though denied room at the inn, are nonetheless protected. By an unworldly, unassuming man and by the other-worldly, invisible power that three wise kings bend to adore.

In this poetic reading, Jesus's birthday becomes a symbol of creative possibility, of what can happen, any moment of our lives, when we acknowledge the invisible, creative life-force within.

That miracle symbolised by christmas happens in a smaller, less acknowledged way every time the five vowel sounds and twenty-one consonants of the English language come together to tell us something true or beautiful about human life on earth, and all that lies within and without it. As in each of the poems in this short book.

The First Day of Christmas: Birthing.
Poem: "The Nativity of our Lord and Saviour Jesus Christ."
By Christopher Smart.

The collection kicks off with the most christian poem, by Christopher Smart, a poet, preacher and *bon viveur* whose religiosity saw him into a lunatic asylum and debtor's prison. Never has the christian take on the mid-winter message been better expressed than in this eulogy, where Smart triumphantly resounds the music and majesty and might of Jesus Christ's weak, meek and lowly birth, its promise to rout "the pow'rs of darkness" in the season of "their utmost gloom".

Poets have always been keener than critics on Smart's work, more appreciative of the craft that separates his poems from the hundreds of thousands of others fired by religious fervour. The scholastic character of Smart's time and place — Augustan London — was, as is much of today's Western world, scientific and "rational". Writers who favoured materialism, the doctrine that nothing exists except what we can "prove", held sway. The religious, even the spiritual-minded, were seen as anti-intellectual, even simple-minded.

For this reason, Peter Porter has described Smart as "the purest case of man's vision prevailing over the spirit of his times." WB Yeats agreed, including Smart's "A Song to David" in his Oxford Book of Modern Verse, introducing it as the poem with which man, "passive before a mechanized nature," began to beat against the door of "his prison". "A Song to David" was the poem that launched the Romantic period, said Yeats.

Yeats, Porter and many other poets — and yes, me too — see Smart as more than somebody who was able to craft a decent eulogy. His ringing reaffirmation of spiritual values in an age of materialism is an act of poetry in itself and his poems, though fervent, take a creative view of his Almighty God that non-theists can identify with.

This is beautifully asserted here in his nativity poem, where he conjoins the natural and supernatural — "Birds on box and laurels listen,/As so near the cherubs hymn". Nature is reflective of the power incarnate within it, an "all-bounteous, all-creative" god whose birth quiets the winds, lights the dark and makes the apparently lifeless winter trees burst into bloom.

Page 15: "The Nativity of our Lord and Saviour." Christopher Smart.

The Second Day of Christmas: Believing.
Poem: "Christmas". By John Betjeman.

But is it true? That's the famous question posed by John Betjeman two centuries later in our own post-Romantic, sceptical times. Can it, asks the twentieth century's poet laureate of middle-England, possibly be true that "the Maker of the stars and sea/ became a Child on earth for me?"

Betjeman, a practicing Anglican who reveals his belief with his christiancapital letters, nonetheless finds it hard to say an unequivocal yes. In another poem he wrote "God grant before we die we all/May see the light as did St. Paul", Paul being, famously, a zealous persecutor of the followers of Jesus who came round to their way of thinking. Betjeman, the practicing Anglican, suffered always from the nagging doubt that plagues any intelligent person about any specific set of beliefs and rituals: is it, is it, is it true?

Francis Bacon, the man credited with popularising the scientific method, once said: "If a man will begin with certainties, he shall end in doubts; but if he will be content to begin with doubts, he shall end in certainties".

Betjeman puts it thus in his christmas poem: If indeed "God was man in Palestine/And lives today in Bread and Wine", if that astonishing verity truly is true, then none of the other displays of the season, the carolling and shopping and decorating and gifting, come close to paying it due honour.

If.

Page 17: "Christmas." John Betjeman.

The Third Day of Christmas: Doubting.
Poem: "The Oxen". By Thomas Hardy

Betjeman clings to his belief in the christmas story, while fearing it false. In our third poem, Thomas Hardy asserts unbelief, while wishing it true.

Hardy began his life as a believer and until his mid-twenties, seriously considered a career in the church but eventually turned atheist. In his christmas poem, he captures the desire for belief that lingers in the most disbelieving soul, by reliving the memory of a country legend passed to him by his mother, and her parents before her. The story goes that the beasts of the field, whose ancestors witnessed the birth of Jesus in Bethlehem, kneel every christmas eve at midnight to commemorate the human birth of god.

The poem begins by recalling how, in Hardy's childhood, sitting by the fire with the adults, it would not have occurred to him or "to one of us there / To doubt" it. He invests the memory with great ease and warmth, then in the third stanza, with an abrupt caesura in the second line, drops us into the contrast of "these years" -- the harsh, disbelieving adult world where "few would weave… so fair a fancy".

These years. Hardy wrote this poem in 1915, the second christmas of the that was supposed to have been over the christmas before, "the war to end all wars" which had, by then, revealed itself in its full, unprecedented, trench-bound horror.

Yet inescapable memory raises its childhood head, even in the face of more than a million deaths. The grown man cannot hold the child's belief in the "fair fancy" at the heart of the christmas story: but, oh, how he longs for it.

Page 19: "The Oxen." By Thomas Hardy.

The Fourth Day of Christmas: Connecting.
Poem: "Christmas Poem". By Mary Oliver.

The same country legend informs Mary Oliver's "Christmas Poem" and Oliver moves us further along the fault-line of longing. "My work is loving the world," Oliver has said and a profound and persistent desire for a joyous union with nature is the signature of this American poet's work, particularly union with the animal world, so this poem — where she literally lies down with the beasts — is emblematic.

For Oliver these cattle, "innocent of history" as "immaculate" as when they first "thundered forth on the morning of creation" are the real miracle. They are no heretics for refusing to kneel at the midnight; rather, they are themselves the christmas spirit incarnate, the thing itself.

That's a story the poet can lie down with, and she does, absorbing their warm presence in the "dissolving now". She is caught in longing for what Bethlehem represents but the beasts, "citizens of the pure… innocent of history" can, if she allows, create for her their own Bethlehem, nuzzle her hair as if she were a child and warm her all through the night.

Page 21: "Christmas Poem." Mary Oliver.

The Fifth Day of Christmas: Sensing.
Poem: "Noel". By Anne Porter.

For Oliver, it is animals that best embody the creative spirit that is the essence of the christmas story. For our next poet, Anne Porter, it is children. Babies. For her, the newborn Jesus is no more a sacred symbol than any newborn.

Porter's poems tend towards the short and unadorned. Like folk songs, or indeed carols, they cut directly to the heart of life, and that heart is always ambiguous. In this poem, she revels in christmas imagery and in the words and sounds and questions it conjures up, year on year, especially that posed by the birth of babies, those "altogether new" arrivals from another world, with their "small limbs/and birdlike voices" begging questions.

Approaching these questions through banal and everyday christmas images -- the trees, the lights, the carols that have gown stale with repetition but are nonetheless loved for reasons of nostalgia -- the poem takes a turn at the start of the fifth stanza on the word "But". We are introduced to the "haunting music/Of the other world" that contrasts with the carols, and the poem becomes a passionate plea to crack the crust of the quotidian to get to the wild, dangerous message of christmas, to connect with its creative heart.

To, in those words of another American poet about poetry, and by implication life: "make it new".

For Porter, a poet who did not take her own talent seriously until after she had raised five children and her husband died, the just born, clear-eyed child raises piercing questions we can only answer if we leave this world and embrace the divine.

Page 23: "Noel." By Anne Porter.

The Sixth Day of Christmas: Seeking.
Poem: "The Magi". By William Butler Yeats.

The "god-shaped question" is also the subject of WB Yeats poem about The Magi, the three men variously called kings or wise men who came to Bethlehem on the night of Jesus's birth to pay homage to a new saviour. For Yeats, they are trapped forever in that posture of searching for that which they can revere. He pictures them "in their stiff, painted clothes... pale [and] unsatisfied...their eyes still fixed," caught in an eternal seeking that will never find what it is looking for.

Yeats, of course, was magus as well as poet and by the time he wrote this poem in 1916, had spent decades seeking answers to the eternal questions, through ancient Irish myth and legend, through magic rituals, through symbolic drama and poetry. At this time, he was also seeking more earthly salvation in the form of a wife and children, an ambition he fulfilled within a few years of writing. By the end of his life, when all he he had ever wanted on the worldly plane was his — wife, daughter, son, old house with grounds Grounds where plum and cabbage grew, and the work done, "something to perfection brought" — he wrote his almost unbearably poignant lines: "What then? sang Plato's ghost. What then?"

In this short poem, he projects onto the wise men his own inability to find consolation in the other plane to which he has devoted his life, which always remains trembling before him, tantalisingly elusive, behind the veil. His kings, undernourished and unconvinced by the "turbulence" of the story of Bethlehem and Calvary, their "eyes still fixed" must pace the heavens too, perpetually unsatisfied.

Page25: "The Magi". W.B. Yeats.

The Seventh Day of Christmas: Travelling.
Poem: "Journey of The Magi". By TS Eliot.

Yeats's near contemporary, TS Eliot, also pictures christmas through the lens of the magi, though his are more human, more physical, occupying a poem full of the mundane details of travel: snow, lack of decent shelter, cursing camel-men, hostile cities and towns, dirty and overcharging villagers, exhaustion and confusion and questioning if "this was all folly".

But then one morning "at dawn", it all becomes worthwhile as they come down into a temperate valley and find what they have been seeking. Written in 1927 shortly after his conversion to Anglican-Catholicism, Eliot has his magus surprised by the consequences of a significant birth. Before this, he "had seen birth and death,/But had thought they were different." What his journey, the physical one, and the political and religious one that followed, taught him was that creation always has destruction embedded within.

Overall, what the magi found and its consequences, a new way of seeing and believing, was, "(you might say) satisfactory". Surely this word, in this poem on the same subject, is an answer to Yeats's "unsatisfied ones"

For though Eliot's magus claims satisfaction, and would do it all again, it is a long way from the traditional joy of christmas and he is still cut off -- his way was on the losing side as new "alien people clutching their gods" saw off "the old dispensation" that favoured him and his kind.

Having journeyed so far, seen too much birth and the death and agony it unleashes, he would be glad of another death, and the implied new birth, that would follow.

Page 27: "Journey Of The Magi." T.S. Eliot.

The Eighth Day of Christmas: Giving.
Poem: "Christmas Time". By Dan Holloway.

It's perhaps unsurprising that Yeats, the aristocracy lover, and Eliot the banker-publisher, the two "great" male poets choose to see the christmas story through the eyes of great men, ignoring the poor and vulnerable woman and child. The poor and vulnerable and all those who live in the shadow side of christmas are the concern of Dan Holloway, a young British poet who has emerged from the vibrant public poetics of slamming and competition.

Holloway is far less concerned with what Yeats calls the "uncontrollable mystery" of christmas than its social and cultural manifestations. Where Betjeman's affectionate 1950s portrait shows us a suburban world where "girls in slacks remember Dad,/And oafish louts remember Mum,/And sleepless children's hearts are glad./And Christmas-morning bells say 'Come!', Holloway's concern is those who are dispossessed, materially and emotionally.

His poem lambastes the British nation's "Christmas box/poptastic toss/and TV dross…" and points the way to how and what those who want to truly give should spend at this time, at all times.

Page 29: "Christmas Time." Dan Holloway.

The Ninth Day of Christmas: Loving.
Poem: "Translations". By Adrienne Rich.

The social order is also the topic of the next poem but here gender is the dispossessor. Jesus, like every other human who ever lived was, in the words of the great Adrienne Rich, "of woman born" and Rich's "Translations" speaks of the politics of female love and despair love as experienced one christmas day, on 25 December 1972.

That the male betrayal which ignites the female epiphany of the poem happens on the traditional day of family loving and giving is essential to the message of the poem. Rich's father was jewish, her mother a southern US protestant, and she was raised christian. Though the day is christmas, the only concession to tradition is a little ivy. Though the scene is domestic -- women fill an oven, bake bread, stir rice, iron a shirt, make a phone call — the atmosphere is harshly cold and and lonely.

At the time of writing, Rich was coming to repudiate the choice society wants us all to make "between 'love' - womanly, maternal love, altruistic love - a love defined and ruled by the weight of an entire culture, and 'egotism' - a force directed by men into creation, achievement, ambition, often at the expense of others.... We know now that the alternatives are false ones - that the word 'love' is itself in need of re-vision."

This poem, in which Rich imagines three women united in needy, female love -- love baked and watched and worn -- depicts in chilling depths this choice that is no choice. The women think their "way of sorrow" is individual, personal, but Rich's short poem brings into living, breathing expression the great feminist insight that the personal is political. So centred are they on this man they both think they love, they fail to see that other is also a loving sister, and fail to hear how their stories speak of, and could speak to, each other.

Page 31: "Translations." Adrienne Rich.

The Tenth Day of Christmas: Mothering
Poem: "Christmas Eve". By Anne Sexton.
In another poem of loneliness and disconnection, we are taken into the searing heart of a complex mother-child relationship. The christmas story has nothing to say to daughters and that is often a source of anger for women poets.

Sexton here captures daughterly anger within agonising imagery and a tightly controlled rhyme scheme and rhythm that slowly unpeels her ambivalence:

your ageing daughters, each one a wife,
each one talking to the family cook,
each one avoiding your portrait,
each one aping your life.

What takes the emotion beyond the poet's individual relationship with her mother into something more universal is its allusion to the christmas story. Her mother's name was also the name of Jesus's mother. In the poem that name is invoked and absolution sought: "Mary-- Mary, Mary, forgive me", as the poet touches her breast, "as if, somehow, it were one of yours."

That "somehow", that ambivalence and inability to understand comes between the poet and what might be her salvation but her torn understanding does not provide a place within which the great christmas message of forgiveness can find a hold, without which creation, a new beginning, cannot arise. The torment of ambivalence cannot be assuaged, the poet is left with "that present that I lost", that she knows she will never find in her dead, sharp diamond of a mother.

This is a very private poem. Such pain is painful to witness and the reader's discomfort is intensified by the knowledge that Sexton ended her own life -- and that on the evening she sat into a closed car and opened the throttle, she was wearing her dead mother's fur coat.

Page 33: "Christmas Eve". Anne Sexton.

The Eleventh Day of Christmas: Remembering
Poem:"A Christmas Childhood". By Patrick Kavanagh.

This is another poem born out of loneliness and solitude. Kavanagh wrote it after spending a festive season alone in his bachelor flat in Dublin and the poem is infused with nostalgia for rural, farm-family life, recalled through the lens of christmas. The memories come dressed in christian imagery, from the story of genesis to the virgin birth.

The first section of the poem sets the scene. The adult Kavanagh recalls the "gay Garden that was childhood's": the frosted potato-pits, the music coming from the paling-post, the heavenly light between ricks of hay and straw, the "December-glinting fruit" on an apple tree. In that Garden of Eden, the most commonplace event -- even "the tracks of cattle to a drinking-place [or] a green stone lying sideways in a ditch" -- was invested with a sense of wonder and love, the "beauty that the world did not touch".

"How wonderful!" says the poet now, longing to return to this creative consciousness that as adult, he can only rarely access now.

In the second part of the poem, he moves more deeply into the memories of one particular christmas year when he was "six Christmases of age", feeling again the fresh and raw wonder of childhood. In the here-and-now moment of adulthood, the act of looking back and capturing the images, provides consolation and reconnects him -- and us -- to the inspiration of christmas and of childhood, enabling us, far away in time and place, to enjoy the melodeon, the music of cows milking and to experience for ourselves our own open, childlike, creative awareness as prayer and blessing: "a white rose pinned on the Virgin's Mary's blouse".

Page 35: "A Christmas Childhood." Patrick Kavanagh.

The Twelfth Day of Christmas:
Poem: "For The Time Being: A Christmas Oratorio".
By W.H. Auden.

The final poem in the collection is a section from the most remarkable christmas poem ever written, "For The Time Being: A Christmas Oratorio", by WH Auden. Composed in 1942, the darkest days from the British Allies perspective of World War II, the poem is 1500 lines long (more than 50 pages), a series of dramatic monologues spoken by the characters of the nativity story, in twentieth-century speech, as if the events were happening in that time.

It's a long parable, merging biblical and contemporary into an audacious display of metaphysical poetics underpinned by Anglican theology.

> *How could the Eternal do a temporal act,*
> *The Infinite become a finite fact?*
> *Nothing can save us that is possible:*
> *We who must die demand a miracle.*

The structure is held together with choruses and a narrator and in the penultimate section anthologised here, christmas is over and its meaning pondered.

Auden's conclusion seems to be that god is always, even in the dead days of January and February, acting "to redeem from insignificance" what we insist on seeing as the monotonous sludge of our everyday life.

The poet knows that rational materialism, Euclid's geometry and Newton's mechanics, will not suffice to explain life to ourselves and so he remakes the christmas story as a story for our time and all time, a story that insists upon god, in the final chorus of section IV, as the way, the truth and the life, now and for all time, that always collapses into the "time being", the here and now.

Page 37: "A Christmas Oratorio". W.H. Auden.

The 1st Day: Birthing

"The Nativity of our Lord and Saviour Jesus Christ."
Christopher Smart.

Where is this stupendous stranger,
Swains of Solyma, advise?
Lead me to my Master's manger,
Show me where my Saviour lies.

O Most Mighty! O MOST HOLY!
Far beyond the seraph's thought,
Art thou then so mean and lowly
As unheeded prophets taught?

O the magnitude of meekness!
Worth from worth immortal sprung;
O the strength of infant weakness,
If eternal is so young!

If so young and thus eternal,
Michael tunc the shepherd's reed,
Where the scenes are ever vernal,
And the loves be Love indeed!

See the God blasphem'd and doubted
In the schools of Greece and Rome;
See the pow'rs of darkness routed,
Taken at their utmost gloom.

Nature's decorations glisten
Far above their usual trim;
Birds on box and laurels listen,
As so near the cherubs hymn.

Boreas now no longer winters
On the desolated coast;
Oaks no more are riv'n in splinters
By the whirlwind and his host.

Spinks and ouzels sing sublimely,
"We too have a Saviour born";
Whiter blossoms burst untimely
On the blest Mosaic thorn.

God all-bounteous, all-creative,
Whom no ills from good dissuade,
Is incarnate, and a native
Of the very world He made.

~ **Christopher Smart**'s "The Nativity of our Lord and Saviour Jesus Christ" was composed while Smart was incarcerated in a mental asylum and published in the collection *Hymns and Spiritual Songs for the Fasts and Festivals of the Church of England* in 1765.

The 2nd Day: Believing

"Christmas." John Betjeman.

The bells of waiting Advent ring,
The Tortoise stove is lit again
And lamp-oil light across the night
Has caught the streaks of winter rain
In many a stained-glass window sheen
From Crimson Lake to Hookers Green.

The holly in the windy hedge
And round the Manor House the yew
Will soon be stripped to deck the ledge,
The altar, font and arch and pew,
So that the villagers can say
'The church looks nice' on Christmas Day.

Provincial Public Houses blaze,
Corporation tramcars clang,
On lighted tenements I gaze,
Where paper decorations hang,
And bunting in the red Town Hall
Says 'Merry Christmas to you all'.

And London shops on Christmas Eve

Are strung with silver bells and flowers
As hurrying clerks the City leave
To pigeon-haunted classic towers,
And marbled clouds go scudding by
The many-steepled London sky.

And girls in slacks remember Dad,
And oafish louts remember Mum,
And sleepless children's hearts are glad.
And Christmas-morning bells say 'Come!'
Even to shining ones who dwell
Safe in the Dorchester Hotel.

And is it true,
This most tremendous tale of all,
Seen in a stained-glass window's hue,
A Baby in an ox's stall ?
The Maker of the stars and sea
Become a Child on earth for me ?

And is it true ? For if it is,
No loving fingers tying strings
Around those tissued fripperies,
The sweet and silly Christmas things,
Bath salts and inexpensive scent
And hideous tie so kindly meant,

No love that in a family dwells,
No carolling in frosty air,
Nor all the steeple-shaking bells
Can with this single Truth compare -
That God was man in Palestine
And lives today in Bread and Wine.

~ **John Betjeman**'s "Christmas" appeared in Collected Poems (1958).

The 3rd Day: Doubting

"The Oxen." By Thomas Hardy.

Christmas Eve, and twelve of the clock.
   "Now they are all on their knees,"
An elder said as we sat in a flock
   By the embers in hearthside ease.

We pictured the meek mild creatures where
   They dwelt in their strawy pen,
Nor did it occur to one of us there
   To doubt they were kneeling then.

So fair a fancy few would weave
   In these years! Yet, I feel,
If someone said on Christmas Eve,
   "Come; see the oxen kneel,

"In the lonely barton by yonder coomb
   Our childhood used to know,"
I should go with him in the gloom,
   Hoping it might be so.

~ **Thomas Hardy**'s "The Oxen" first appeared in *The Times* (London) on 24th December 1915.

The 4th Day: Connecting

"Christmas Poem." Mary Oliver.

Says a country legend told every year:
Go to the barn on Christmas Eve and see
what the creatures do as that long night tips over.
Down on their knees they will go, the fire
of an old memory whistling through their minds!

So I went. Wrapped to my eyes against the cold
I creaked back the barn door and peered in.
From town the church bells spilled their midnight music,
and the beasts listened – yet they lay in their stalls like stone.

Oh the heretics!
Not to remember Bethlehem,
or the star as bright as a sun,
or the child born on a bed of straw!
To know only of the dissolving Now!

Still they drowsed on –
citizens of the pure, the physical world,
they loomed in the dark: powerful
of body, peaceful of mind, innocent of history.

Brothers! I whispered. *It is Christmas!*
And you are no heretics, but a miracle,
immaculate still as when you thundered forth
on the morning of creation!
As for Bethlehem, that blazing star

still sailed the dark, but only looked for me.
Caught in its light, listening again to its story,
I curled against some sleepy beast, who nuzzled
my hair as though I were a child, and warmed me
the best it could all night.

~ **Mary Oliver**'s "Christmas Poem" appeared in: Swan: Poems and Prose Poems, Beacon (Boston, MA), 2010.

The 5th Day: Sensing

"Noel." By Anne Porter.

When snow is shaken
From the balsam trees
And they're cut down
And brought into our houses

When clustered sparks
Of many-colored fire
Appear at night
In ordinary windows

We hear and sing
The customary carols

They bring us ragged miracles
And hay and candles
And flowering weeds of poetry
That are loved all the more
Because they are so common

But there are carols
That carry phrases
Of the haunting music

Of the other world
A music wild and dangerous
As a prophet's message

Or the fresh truth of children
Who though they come to us
From our own bodies
Are altogether new
With their small limbs
And birdlike voices

They look at us
With their clear eyes
And ask the piercing questions
God alone can answer.

~ **Anne Porter**'s "Noel" was first published in *Living Things: Collected Poems* (2006)

The 6th Day: Seeking

"The Magi". W.B. Yeats.

Now as at all times I can see in the mind's eye,
In their stiff, painted clothes, the pale unsatisfied ones
Appear and disappear in the blue depth of the sky
With all their ancient faces like rain-beaten stones,
And all their helms of silver hovering side by side,
And all their eyes still fixed, hoping to find once more,
Being by Calvary's turbulence unsatisfied,
The uncontrollable mystery on the bestial floor.

~ **William Butler Yeats**'s "The Magi" was published in *Responsibilities* 1916.

The 7th Day: Travelling

"Journey Of The Magi." T.S. Eliot.

'A cold coming we had of it,
Just the worst time of the year
For a journey, and such a long journey:
The ways deep and the weather sharp,
The very dead of winter.'
And the camels galled, sorefooted, refractory,
Lying down in the melting snow.
There were times we regretted
The summer palaces on slopes, the terraces,
And the silken girls bringing sherbet.
Then the camel men cursing and grumbling
and running away, and wanting their liquor and women,
And the night-fires going out, and the lack of shelters,
And the cities hostile and the towns unfriendly
And the villages dirty and charging high prices:
A hard time we had of it.
At the end we preferred to travel all night,
Sleeping in snatches,
With the voices singing in our ears, saying
That this was all folly.

Then at dawn we came down to a temperate valley,
Wet, below the snow line, smelling of vegetation;

With a running stream and a water-mill beating the darkness,
And three trees on the low sky,
And an old white horse galloped away in the meadow.
Then we came to a tavern with vine-leaves over the lintel,
Six hands at an open door dicing for pieces of silver,
And feet kiking the empty wine-skins.
But there was no information, and so we continued
And arriving at evening, not a moment too soon
Finding the place; it was (you might say) satisfactory.

All this was a long time ago, I remember,
And I would do it again, but set down
This set down
This: were we led all that way for
Birth or Death? There was a Birth, certainly
We had evidence and no doubt. I had seen birth and death,
But had thought they were different; this Birth was
Hard and bitter agony for us, like Death, our death.
We returned to our places, these Kingdoms,
But no longer at ease here, in the old dispensation,
With an alien people clutching their gods.
I should be glad of another death.

~ **T.S.Eliot**'s "Journey of the Magi," the first in a series of poems later grouped as the Ariel Poems, was published in 1927.

The 8th Day: Giving

"Christmas Time." Dan Holloway.

This is the season of the dying and the dead
The poorly fed and those that life misled,
Of keening dread and unheard screaming in their head
And suicide notes that go unread
This is the season of the dying and the dead
The names that no one knows
A nation's blinded conscience painted red upon the snow.

Through unpulled curtains,
Yellow nets
Through sherry vodka and regrets
We watch a nation with its Christmas box –
Poptastic toss
And TV dross
And things designed to remind you of your loss

Stocking lines of dreams and hopes
Are folded down to cards and enveloped
Posted and forgotten like the Christmas roast
Children's smiles
Remind the childless of the mindless chance of life
Its idle dance while idols rise from circumstance

Don't spare a thought for those
Who wake alone, turn on the lights alone
And watch TV and eat,
Put out the lights and go to sleep at night alone
And while they might be out of sight alone
You never ask if they're all right alone
You just bemoan the family fights
And wish that you could spend one night alone
Watching Twilight alone
Well, quite alone,
It's not like you'd like to share their plight alone.
Don't spare a line at a slam or a rhyme
Or prayers to non-existent gods when mass bells chime.
If you want to give.
If you want to stop the clocks,
To put the slow tick tock of grown men's loneliness in stocks
And let them live…
Give
Time

~ **Dan Holloway**'s "Christmas Time" was initially written for the Cirencester Christmas Slam 2011.

The 9th Day: Loving

"Translations." Adrienne Rich.

December 25, 1972
You show me the poems of some woman
my age, or younger
translated from your language
Certain words occur: enemy, oven, sorrow
enough to let me know
she's a woman of my time
obsessed
with Love, our subject:
we've trained it like ivy to our walls
baked it like bread in our ovens
worn it like lead on our ankles
watched it through binoculars as if
it were a helicopter
bringing food to our famine
or the satellite
of a hostile power
I begin to see that woman
doing things: stirring rice
ironing a skirt
typing a manuscript till dawn
trying to make a call

from a phone-booth
The phone rings endlessly
in a man's bedroom
she hears him telling someone else
Never mind. She'll get tired.
hears him telling her story to her sister
who becomes her enemy
and will in her own way
light her own way to sorrow
ignorant of the fact this way of grief
is shared, unnecessary
and political.

~ **Adrienne Rich**'s "Translations" was written on Christmas Day 1972 and first published in *Diving Into The Wreck*.

The 10th Day: Mothering

"Christmas Eve." Anne Sexton.

Oh sharp diamond, my mother!
I could not count the cost
of all your faces, your moods--
that present that I lost.
Sweet girl, my deathbed,
my jewel-fingered lady,
your portrait flickered all night
by the bulbs of the tree.

Your face as calm as the moon
over a mannered sea,
presided at the family reunion,
the twelve grandchildren
you used to wear on your wrist,
a three-months-old baby,
a fat check you never wrote,
the red-haired toddler who danced the twist,
your aging daughters, each one a wife,
each one talking to the family cook,
each one avoiding your portrait,
each one aping your life.

Later, after the party,
after the house went to bed,

I sat up drinking the Christmas brandy,
watching your picture,
letting the tree move in and out of focus.
The bulbs vibrated.
They were a halo over your forehead.
Then they were a beehive,
blue, yellow, green, red;
each with its own juice, each hot and alive
stinging your face. But you did not move.
I continued to watch, forcing myself,
waiting, inexhaustible, thirty-five.

I wanted your eyes, like the shadows
of two small birds, to change.
But they did not age.
The smile that gathered me in, all wit,
all charm, was invincible.
Hour after hour I looked at your face
but I could not pull the roots out of it.
Then I watched how the sun hit your red sweater, your withered neck,
your badly painted flesh-pink skin.
You who led me by the nose, I saw you as you were.
Then I thought of your body
as one thinks of murder--

Then I said Mary--
Mary, Mary, forgive me
and then I touched a present for the child,
the last I bred before your death;
and then I touched my breast
and then I touched the floor
and then my breast again as if,
somehow, it were one of yours.

~ **Anne Sexton**'s "Christmas Eve" was written in 1964 and first published in the collection, *Live Or Die*.

The 11th Day: Remembering

"A Christmas Childhood." Patrick Kavanagh.

One side of the potato-pits was white with frost--
How wonderful that was, how wonderful!
And when we put our ears to the paling-post
The music that came out was magical.
The light between the ricks of hay and straw
Was a hole in Heaven's gable. An apple tree
With its December-glinting fruit we saw--
O you, Eve, were the world that tempted me
To eat the knowledge that grew in clay
And death the germ within it! Now and then
I can remember something of the gay
Garden that was childhood's. Again
The tracks of cattle to a drinking-place,
A green stone lying sideways in a ditch
Or any common sight the transfigured face
Of a beauty that the world did not touch.

II

My father played the melodeon
Outside at our gate;
There were stars in the morning east

And they danced to his music.
Across the wild bogs his melodeon called
To Lennons and Callans.
As I pulled on my trousers in a hurry
I knew some strange thing had happened.
Outside the cow-house my mother
Made the music of milking;
The light of her stable-lamp was a star
And the frost of Bethlehem made it twinkle.
A water-hen screeched in the bog,
Mass-going feet
Crunched the wafer-ice on the pot-holes,
Somebody wistfully twisted the bellows wheel.
My child poet picked out the letters
On the grey stone,
In silver the wonder of a Christmas townland,
The winking glitter of a frosty dawn.
Cassiopeia was over
Cassidy's hanging hill,
I looked and three whin bushes rode across
The horizon. The Three Wise Kings.
An old man passing said:
'Can't he make it talk'--
The melodeon. I hid in the doorway
And tightened the belt of my box-pleated coat.
I nicked six nicks on the door-post
With my penknife's big blade.
There was a little one for cutting tobacco,
And I was six Christmases of age.
My father played the melodeon,
My mother milked the cows,
And I had a prayer like a white rose pinned
On the Virgin Mary's blouse.

~ **Patrick Kavanagh**'s "A Christmas Childhood" was first published in The Irish Press on 24th December 1943.

The 12th Day: Enduring

From "For The Time Being: A Christmas Oratorio". W.H. Auden.

III
Narrator

Well, so that is that. Now we must dismantle the tree,
Putting the decorations back into their cardboard boxes --
Some have got broken -- and carrying them up to the attic.
The holly and the mistletoe must be taken down and burnt,
And the children got ready for school. There are enough
Left-overs to do, warmed-up, for the rest of the week --
Not that we have much appetite, having drunk such a lot,
Stayed up so late, attempted -- quite unsuccessfully --
To love all of our relatives, and in general
Grossly overestimated our powers. Once again
As in previous years we have seen the actual Vision and failed
To do more than entertain it as an agreeable
Possibility, once again we have sent Him away,
Begging though to remain His disobedient servant,
The promising child who cannot keep His word for long.
The Christmas Feast is already a fading memory,
And already the mind begins to be vaguely aware
Of an unpleasant whiff of apprehension at the thought
Of Lent and Good Friday which cannot, after all, now

Be very far off. But, for the time being, here we all are,
Back in the moderate Aristotelian city
Of darning and the Eight-Fifteen, where Euclid's geometry
And Newton's mechanics would account for our experience,
And the kitchen table exists because I scrub it.
It seems to have shrunk during the holidays. The streets
Are much narrower than we remembered; we had forgotten
The office was as depressing as this. To those who have seen
The Child, however dimly, however incredulously,
The Time Being is, in a sense, the most trying time of all.
For the innocent children who whispered so excitedly
Outside the locked door where they knew the presents to be
Grew up when it opened. Now, recollecting that moment
We can repress the joy, but the guilt remains conscious;
Remembering the stable where for once in our lives
Everything became a You and nothing was an It.
And craving the sensation but ignoring the cause,
We look round for something, no matter what, to inhibit
Our self-reflection, and the obvious thing for that purpose
Would be some great suffering. So, once we have met the Son,
We are tempted ever after to pray to the Father;
"Lead us into temptation and evil for our sake."
They will come, all right, don't worry; probably in a form
That we do not expect, and certainly with a force
More dreadful than we can imagine. In the meantime
There are bills to be paid, machines to keep in repair,
Irregular verbs to learn, the Time Being to redeem
From insignificance. The happy morning is over,
The night of agony still to come; the time is noon:
When the Spirit must practice his scales of rejoicing
Without even a hostile audience, and the Soul endure
A silence that is neither for nor against her faith
That God's Will will be done, That, in spite of her prayers,
God will cheat no one, not even the world of its triumph.

IV

Chorus:
He is the Way.
Follow Him through the Land of Unlikeness;
You will see rare beasts, and have unique adventures.
He is the Truth.
Seek Him in the Kingdom of Anxiety;
You will come to a great city that has expected your return for years.
He is the Life.
Love Him in the World of the Flesh;
And at your marriage all its occasions shall dance for joy

~ **W. H. Auden**'s "Christmas Oratorio" was written 1941-42 and first published in 1944.

Conclusion: Blessing

And so we come full circle to the truth and the way, christmas as poetic symbol for the metaphysical time that collapses clock time, the metaphysical place that defies earth-bound materialism: the hallowed space that christians call union, that Buddhists call enlightenment, that sufis call *fana*: the self-forgetting absorption into the creative force that underlies all phenomena, where all is calm, all is bright.

Another word for it is love, not the romantic kind, or the sentimental kind that sometimes saccharines the mid-winter feast, but the love that Emily Dickinson described as "anterior to life, posterior to death, initial of creation and the exponent of breath". The great, open creative space that both births everything on earth and is itself birthed each time anything is made manifest.

Yes, christmas can be a crass, materialist, over-sentimentalised holiday, that rides roughshod over other belief systems, but without the earthbound existence where we are frail and ill and broken and bad, we cannot know the joys of heavenly peace. They interpenetrate. In the words of the well-known poet and Zen master, Thich Nhat Hanh, they *inter-are*.

Or as another poet, Leonard Cohen, puts it: "There is a crack in everything. That's how the light gets in."

All the signifiers of light within darkness that humans have celebrated in mid-winter point to that place beyond place, the time-out-of-time where I hope you'll spend most of your holiday season.

I'd like to finish by offering a poem from another tradition, a tradition that absorbed christian ideas and melded them with old, pagan ways into a belief system and social structure that, because of its isolation on the edge of an island on the edge of Europe, stayed intact in Ireland well into the twentieth century.

These ancient traditions of roving and hospitality that date from before the birth at Bethlehem were still at play in the Irish village where I grew up in the 1960s. I remember them well and with great fondness and have adapted this simple mid-winter blessing that is very ancient but that praises aspects of christmas that believers and nonbelievers and freethinkers can all unite around still today: conviviality, hospitality, giving, pleasure. All the outer signifiers of inner joy.

May you have a happy and wholesome holiday season and a glorious new year, that has many blessings, including a poem to love, in each and every day of it.

"Mid-Winter Benediction."
Orna Ross.

Father, mother, growing child,
all blessings on you all.
Bless your hearth, and bless your board,
and every sturdy wall.

Bless the fields about your place,
the hillock and the sedge.
Bless holly bush and laurel
and birdsong from the hedge.
Bless the air on hands and face,
and sun on winter's day.
Bless trees that broke the gnaw of wind,
and heralded the way.
Bless your two open windows
letting moon and starlight in.
Bless unlatched door that welcomed
a stranger as if kin.
Bless the roof that shelters you,
the cribs on which you rest,
bless the holding of your house,
yes, all your lintels blessed.

Bless bow and fiddle tuning now,
for carols soon to sing.
Bless drink to fire some dancing,
and fire to warm the skin.
Bless news fetched in by neighbours,
all tidings that they bring,
bless feast laid out for feasting,
let merriment begin.
Bless the joy here gathering,
Its life within us ring,
Oh, bless the heart and soul
of every living, blessed thing.

Blessed the hearth, and blessed the board,
and blessed each sturdy wall.
Mother, father, growing child,
all blessings on you all.

~ **Orna Ross**'s "Mid-Winter Benediction" first appeared on her Author Blog, Christmas Eve, 2012.

About The Poets

W. H. Auden was born in York, England in 1907 and died in Vienna, Austria in 1973.
Further Reading: *The Collected Poetry of W. H. Auden.* (1945).

John Betjeman was born in London, England in 1906 and died in Trebetherick, England in 1984.
Further Reading: *Collected Poems.* (1958)

T.S.Eliot was Born in St. Louis, Missouri in 1888 and died in London, England in 1965.
Further Reading: *Collected Poems.* (2009)

Thomas Hardy was born in Stinsford, England in1840 and died at Dorchester, England in 1928.
Further Reading: *Collected Poems.* (1932)

Dan Holloway was born in Salisbury, England in 1971.
Further Reading: *i cannot bring myself to look at walls in case you have graffitied them with love poetry.*

Patrick Kavanagh was born in Monaghan, Ireland in 1904 and died in Dublin in 1967.
Further Reading: *Collected Poems.* (1974).

Mary Oliver was born in Cleveland, Ohio in 1935.
Further Reading: Swan: *Poems and Prose Poems*. (2010).

Anne Porter was born in Sherborn, Massachusetts in 1911 and died at Long Island, New York, in 2011.
Further Reading: Living Things: *Collected Poems*. (2006)

Adrienne Rich was born in Baltimore, Maryland in 1929 and died in Santa Cruz, California in
2012
Further Reading: *Collected Poems*. (1993).

Orna Ross was born in Waterford, Ireland in 1960.
Further Reading: *Ten Thoughts About Love I & II & III* (2011 & 2012 & 2013).

Anne Sexton was born in Newton, Massachusetts in 1928 and died in Weston, Massachusetts in 1974.
Further Reading: *The Complete Poems*. (1981)

Christopher Smart was born in Shipbourne, England in 1722 and died in London, England in 1771.
Further Reading: *Selected Poems*. (1980)

William Butler Yeats was born in Dublin, Ireland in 1865 and died at Merton France in 1939.
Further Reading: *Collected Poems*. (1996)

About The Editor

Orna Ross was born in Waterford, Ireland and now lives in London.

She writes novels, poems and the Go Creative! Books and is Founder and Director of the Alliance of Independent Authors.

Copyright: Introduction © 2013 Orna Ross;
Poems © Individual poets
ISBN EBOOK: 978-0-9573412-2-7
ISBN PBOOK POD: 978-0-9573412-8-9

Font Publications

Font Publications, London, UK.
Enquiries: Contact form on Author-Publisher's website:
www.ornaross.com

Other Books By Orna Ross

Books Published & Forthcoming.
For more information: www.ornaross.com

NOVELS

The Secret Rose: The Yeats-Gonne Trilogy I: Maud & Willie.
A Child Dancing: The Yeats-Gonne Trilogy II: Willie & Iseult.
But A Dream: The Yeats-Gonne Trilogy III, Iseult & Maud.
Blue Mercy.
After The Rising: The Civil War Trilogy I
Before The Fall: The Civil War Trilogy II
In The Hour: The Civil War Trilogy III (forthcoming)

POEMS

Ten Thoughts About Love: Poetry I
Ten More Thoughts About Love: Poetry II
Ten More Thoughts About Love: Poetry III

THE GO CREATIVE! SERIES
Go Creative! It's Your Native State (Process)
Inspiration Meditation:
A Meditation To Ignite Insights & Ideas (Practice)
F-R-E-E-Writing: Unblocking Life's Flow (Practice)
Expressive Exercise: Moving With Life (Practice)
How To Write Haiku: Poems For Creative Presence (Presence)
Creating Money, Creating Meaning:
Getting Into Financial Flow (Process)
The Seven Stages of The Creative Process (Process)
You're Not Crazy, You're Creative (Presence)

THE ALLIANCE OF INDEPENDENT AUTHOR GUIDES
Guides to Author-Publishing: On Writing,
Publishing and Selling Books.
See http://allianceindependentauthors.org for more details.